ROCK TALK™ RULES

Book 1 (The Vowels)
Basic Grammar and Phonics Through Music

Second Edition

Written by Jenny Redding

*Music Produced by Chas Ferry,
Roy Scoutz and Jenny Redding*

Rock Talk, Inc.
Simi Valley, California

Acknowledgments

Special Thanks Goes To
Linda C. Hansen, UCLA Extension, TESOL Certification Program
Dan Fichtner, UCLA Extension, TESOL Certification Program
Eleanor Black, UCLA Extension, TESOL Certification Program
Kathleen Flynn, Glendale Community College
Mike Miller, President, Miller Educational Materials
And the students of Glendale Community College, who sang and sang
And to the students of Oxnard College, who also sang and sang and sang
and especially to UCLA Extension, TESOL Certification Program,
Roy Scoutz (for all the beautiful music), Daniel Dale (for the drums),
Chris Schendel (for the Quark lessons),
Kris Skaie, Jim Manzie, Mike Doman (the singers),
and my husband,
Chas Ferry, for his endless patience
and hard work. Thank you all!

ISBN: 1-930122-05-5 = Book/Tape Set
ISBN: 1-930122-06-3 = Book/CD Set
ISBN: 1-930122-07-1 = Book Only
ISBN: 1-930122-08-X = Tape Only
ISBN: 1-930122-09-8 = CD Only

For Further Information
Please Contact
Jenny Redding or Chas Ferry
c/o Rock Talk, Inc.
1197C E. Los Angeles Avenue, #277
Simi Valley, California 93065
(805) 583-3600 (voice)
Toll Free: (888) 890-4009 (voice)
Fax: (805) 955-9820
E-mail: jenny@eslrocks.com
Website: http://www.eslrocks.com

TABLE of CONTENTS

Ms. Redding was partially deaf until the age of 6 when an operation restored her hearing. From that moment on, she has been fascinated with every aspect of language production and has a keen sensitivity regarding intonation and stress patterns, facial expression and gesture. Shortly after her ear operation, Ms. Redding became an actress at the age of 8. This love for theatre has persisted, as she earned her B.A. in Theatre Arts from UCLA and is currently a Screen Actors Guild member, having worked in television and film. Ms. Redding also earned an M.A. in English Literature from UCLA, as well as her TESOL Certificate. In 1985, Ms. Redding began to develop her talents as a singer/songwriter. By 1988 she was a member of the National Academy of Songwriters and her songs

have been recorded by such artists as Tanya Tucker and Kimberly Carter. In 1995, Ms. Redding (aka Jenny James) released her own original country CD to critical acclaim. Many of the songs are played on Dr. Laura Schlessinger's nationally-syndicated talk show on KFI.

In addition to having a fervent love for theatre arts, singing and songwriting, Jenny's interest in languages has also been a lifelong love. She spent her childhood in Japan. Her family then moved to San Diego, California, where Ms. Redding was engulfed in the Latino culture. She studied Spanish in high school and college and has since recorded original songs in Spanish. Ms. Redding has taught English as a Second Language to adults for over 15 years, both at the community college level and in adult school situations. Her students have ranged from beginners to advanced ESL college students.

All of these talents have coalesced to form the wonderful musical English as a Second Language Series entitled "Rock Talk."

Ms. Redding's partner, Chas Ferry, is a professional record producer and recording engineer. Chas worked at Cherokee Recording Studios throughout the 1980's and has worked with the likes of Steve Perry (of "Journey"), David Bowie and Tin Machine, Rod Stewart, Iggy Pop, Little Richard and Eddie Murphy. Chas has mixed soundtracks for many films including "Eve's Bayou," "American Me," and "Innerspace," to name a few. Before taking over day-to-day operations of Rock Talk, Inc., Chas was working with Christopher Franke, formerly of "Tangerine Dream," as music editor, and musical assistant for "Babylon V," "The Amazing Race," "No Opportunity Wasted," "Pacific Blue," and numerous other television and film productions. Between Chas' recording talents and Ms. Redding's vocal gifts, "Rock Talk" is a pure musical delight and a fresh approach to learning English.

GUIDELINES FOR USING "ROCK TALK"™
(Both for Teacher and Student)

The following are some guidelines to assist both the student and teacher in successfully using "Rock Talk"™ to enhance listening and speaking skills:

*1. **Use "Rock Talk"™ as a Supplement:** "Rock Talk"™ is not meant to be used as a solo teaching strategy; rather, it is best utilized as a **supplement** to already existing curriculum, as well as methodologies, such as Total Physical Response and Cooperative Learning Strategies. For optimal use, only complete one section of a chapter in any given 30-minute period. This gives the learner an opportunity to really listen to the music and adequately complete recommended steps outlined in the <u>Workbook</u>. Also, the sections of each chapter, as well as exercises within sections, are coded as to appropriate learning level, "I" for beginning, "II" for intermediate, and "III" for advanced.*

*2. **Vocal Placement:** To achieve the proper placement of the voice, the singing should be as **pharyngeal** (or nasal) as possible. Teachers should encourage their students to sing in an "ugly" sounding voice (ala "The Wicked Witch of the West"). This "ugly" sound pulls the resonance to the proper place and a more native accent can thereby be achieved.*

*3. **Breathing:** Non-native speakers tend to break up their English sentences into small phrases. By having students **breathe only when the singer on the "Rock Talk"™ tapes breathes**, "Rock Talk"™ directly addresses this issue and helps to enhance student fluency.*

*4. **Various Learning Styles:** Because each chapter incorporates visual elements, audio-linguistic elements, kinesthetic aspects and inter- and intra-personal activities, the <u>Workbook</u> caters to many of the various learning styles, as well as varying levels.*

*5. **Self-Confidence:** Ultimately, we all know that speaking is easier for most people than is singing. Hence, "Rock Talk"™ uses reverse psychology. By "tricking" people into singing, students ultimately find that **speaking** English by comparison is a "breeze." Once self-confidence is raised, students overcome their fear of speaking and are therefore well on their way to achieving communicative competence.*

GUIDELINES — (continued)

6. <u>*Musculature and Gesture:*</u> *Teachers should encourage their students to use their faces, as many non-native speakers are reluctant to do so, probably due to cultural concerns, as well as shyness while learning a new language. If teachers encourage students to make lots of facial expressions (as they might imagine a chimpanzee would), this helps enormously to* **relax** *the facial muscles while simultaneously creating a relaxed and fun atmosphere. Facial muscles are then toned and a more native accent can be achieved.*

7. <u>*Intonation:*</u> *Intonation issues are addressed directly through "Rock Talk's"™* **melody** *focus. The students should try to sing the melodies reflected by the singer on the tapes as much as possible. Students will thereby "absorb" some of the natural intonations of American English as embedded in the "Rock Talk"™ songs.*

8. <u>*Stress:*</u> *The steady drum beat creates a familiar and ever-present rhythm to the "Rock Talk"™ tapes. A teacher can emphasize this* **rhythm** *via kinesthetic means (i.e., having students clap, for example). We also recommend that students walk to the rhythm or stamp their feet as they sing. This all helps reinforce the rhythmic elements of the English language as captured in "Rock Talk's"™ song selections.*

9. <u>*Positive Visualization Techniques:*</u> *For the most effective use of the "Rock Talk"™ method, we recommend that positive visualization techniques also be used in conjunction with the "Rock Talk"™ tapes and <u>Workbook</u> series. This assists students in seeing themselves* **successfully** *enhancing their speaking and listening skills.*

10. <u>*Self-Monitoring:*</u> *When students are working at home with the tapes, in order to* **hear themselves** *clearly as they sing, they should cup their hands behind their ears and bend their ears forward. This enhances the sound and enables students to monitor their own progress at home.*

RATIONALE FOR USING "ROCK TALK"™

Based on the same principles that make popular music popular, "Rock Talk"™ implants melodies and words into students' brains such that the words and melodies just keep going 'round and 'round in their heads. Just like commercial jingles sell products because people get "hooked" in—"Rock Talk"™ strengthens the student's unconscious assimilation of English intonation, rhythm, and even structure. Supported by current brain research, music plays a much greater role in the language acquisition process than previously thought. Brain research supports the idea that emotions play a key role in the storage and recall of information, and music intrinsically evokes emotion. Also, the repetitive nature of popular/rock music further reinforces content aspects of instruction. Furthermore, music by its very nature, can lower the affective filter, if chosen wisely and presented in an attractive, professional manner. Add humor and upbeat tempos, and "Rock Talk"™ provides a winning combination for enhancing the language acquisition process.

"Rock Talk"™ also combines six of the seven pedagogical principles suggested by Yvonne and David Freeman in their book, <u>Whole Language for Second Language Learners</u>. First, "Rock Talk"™ encompasses the concept of teaching from whole to part by first introducing songs in their genuine form. Second, the curriculum is learner-centered. Third, because songs are taken from popular American culture, the lessons have purpose and meaning for the students now. Fourth, as students sing and work together, they engage in social interaction. Fifth, using both the <u>Workbook</u> and tape, these lessons develop both oral and written language skills. Sixth, "Rock Talk"™ intrinsically reflects a faith in the learner's ability to break through the fossilization of his or her pronunciation problems.

Ultimately, music is a universal language that speaks to the depths of the human experience. According to Don Campbell in his book, <u>Introduction to the Musical Brain</u>, "There is something about music's power to invoke and express that is not found in [other] verbal or written forms."

Hi! My name is "Rock Talk." I want to explain to you how to use this program. Each vowel sound is introduced with a warmup song that is simple and repetitive. We then use a fun pop/rock song that focuses specifically on the vowel sound we introduced. Each song in this book is only five or six minutes long. It's so you can practice English in a few minutes a day. They're crazy songs and we hope you love them as much as we do! Have fun!

These exercises are to help familiarize you with English vowel sounds and to help you become more fluent. This should help you become more confident in your English pronunciation. Just remember to breathe when the singer breathes. Also, use an ugly voice, like a witch! This will help you sound more like a native speaker of English. It'll sound ugly to you, but that's good to us! Oh! Remember to snap your fingers, to clap your hands, and to move your body. Your body is learning English, too! Finally, we work on the grammar that is contained in these fun songs as well. Just relax, and after you've been singing for a while, you'll speak English perfectly! See ya!

RULE #1: JUST HAVE FUN
with Short "A"

I. Breaking the Ice Sure Feels Nice

Someone asked me about the sound of the short "a" vowel. "That's easy," I answered. The short "a" is the vowel in "cat" or "hat" or baseball "bat." Let's practice that!

<u>ROCK TALK REALLY ROCKS</u>

The other day I met a man
We said "hello" and then shook hands
He taught me the Rock Talk dance
To move real fast and take a chance

<u>Chorus</u>:
Rock Talk
Rock Talk
Rock Talk really rocks!
Rock Talk really rocks!

You stomp your feet and
   you wiggle* your back
Left, right, left, it goes like that
It'll spin you around 'til it knocks you flat**
It's really fun and that's a fact
[Chorus]

*wiggle=move

**knocks you flat=until you fall down

II. What Does It Mean, Jelly Bean?

I'm Madelyn. But you can call me "Mad" if you would rather! I work for Dr. Rad in a lab. I sat and wrote about that last January!

I work in a lab.  I'm very glad

L _ _

I work in a lab. It's the nicest job I've

ever had. I drive my van  to

V _ _

the lab. And in my van I carry a

map.  And next to my map

M _ _

I have a fan.  And next to that is

F _ _

my pet rat. He is getting

R _ _

kind of fat. I also have a pet cat.

C _ _

She is friends with my pet bat.

B _ _

And next to that

is my backpack.

Tell me what you **B** _ _ _ _ _ _ _

think of that!!

III. Write Your Own Tune, Man in the Moon

My name is Nan Chan and I play tambourine in a band! I want to teach you a simple song called "A Ram Sam Sam" which has the short "a" vowel sound, just like in my name: Nan Chan.

<u>A RAM SAM SAM</u>

A Ram Sam Sam A Ram Sam Sam
Goolie Goolie Goolie Goolie Goolie
Ram Sam Sam

Now, let's add new vocabulary to "A Ram Sam Sam" and it'll be fantastic! Use only short "a" words. You can use the Rhyming Dictionary if you can't think of your own short "a" words!

<u>Rhyming Dictionary</u>	
pan	can
cap	trap
ham	yam

A _____ ____ _____
A _____ ____ _____
Goolie Goolie Goolie
   Goolie Goolie

_____ ____ _____

IV. Movin' and Groovin'

Listen to "The Monster Mash" and dance, dance, dance.

THE MONSTER MASH

Verse #1

I was working in the lab
   late one night
When my eyes beheld an eerie sight
For my monster from his slab began to rise
And suddenly to my surprise

Chorus

He did the Mash
He did the Monster Mash
The Monster Mash
It was a graveyard smash*
He did the Mash
It caught on in a flash**
He did the Mash
He did the Monster Mash

*smash=success

**flash=moment

Verse #2

From my laboratory in the castle east
To the master bedroom where the vampires feast
The ghouls all came from their humble abodes*
To get a jolt** from my electrodes

Chorus

They did the Mash
They did the Monster Mash . . .

Bridge

The zombies were having fun
The party had just begun
The guests included Wolf Man
Dracula and his son

Verse #3

The scene was rockin'
   All were digging the sounds
Igor on chains,
   Backed by his baying*** hounds
The coffin-bangers were about to arrive
With their vocal group,
   "The Crypt-Kicker Five."

*abodes=homes

**jolt=shock

***baying=barking

[Chorus]
They did the Mash
They did the Monster Mash . . .

Verse #4
Out from his coffin, Drac's voice did ring
Seems he was troubled by just one thing
He opened the lid and shook his fist
And said, "Whatever happened
   to my Transylvania Twist?"*

*Transylvania Twist = a dance

Chorus
It's now the Mash . . .

Verse #5
Now everything's cool
Drac's a part of the band
And my Monster Mash is the hit of the land
For you the living this Mash was meant to
When you get to my door
Tell them, "Boris" sent you!

Chorus
Then you can Mash . . .

Which words in "The Monster Mash" have the short "a" vowel sound, like the vowel sound in the word "hand"?

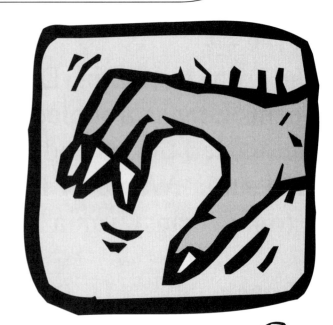

1. _____

2. _____

3. _____

4. _____

5. _____

6. _____

7. _____

8. _____

9. _____

10. _____

11. _____

12. _____

Say these words and try to sound as ugly as you can—like a witch. That's right my honey lamb—my apple jam! See if you can.

9

V. HAMMER THE GRAMMAR

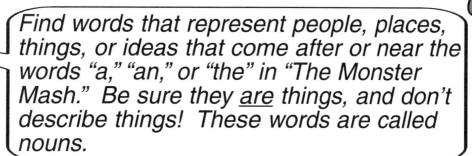

Find words that represent people, places, things, or ideas that come after or near the words "a," "an," or "the" in "The Monster Mash." Be sure they <u>are</u> things, and don't describe things! These words are called nouns.

1. _____   11. _____

2. _____   12. _____

3. _____   13. _____

4. _____   14. _____

5. _____   15. _____

6. _____   16. _____

7. _____   17. _____

8. _____   18. _____

9. _____   19. _____

10. _____   20. _____

Now, find the nouns that follow the word "one":

1. _____   2. _____

Finally, find the nouns that come after or near words such as "my," "his," "her," "your," "their" or "our." List them below. By the way, how do we make nouns plural? That's right! Normally we add "s" or "es." If you want to know more about irregular plural nouns, refer to pages 90-92.

1. _____

2. _____

3. _____

4. _____

5. _____

6. _____

7. _____

8. _____

9. _____

10. _____

11. _____

12. _____

13. _____

14. _____

Another form of a noun (a person, place, thing, or idea), is a Proper Noun, or, the real name of a person, like my name: Madelyn Macks. What "names" or Proper Nouns are mentioned in "The Monster Mash"?

1. _____

2. _____

3. _____

4. _____

11

VI. Hunky Dory, Finish the Story

Fill in the blanks in the following story. Use words you've seen in this Chapter for the short "a" if you can. If not, use your own words.

Once upon a time, in a land far far away, lived a _____. He had long, pointy teeth, and he liked to bite people's necks. He lived in a _____ up on a hill. He had a special room there where he did experiments. That was his _____.

One night he decided to have a party. He even paid a _____ to play his favorite rock 'n roll hits. So many ghosts and goblins came to his party that his neighbors decided they were going to call the police. Luckily, _____, the host, invited them, too. So, they decided not to call the police after all. A _____ even came to pick them up and take them up the hill to the party.

At the door, a butler ghost gave each guest a name _____ to wear. The butler took all the guests' coats and _____, and put them upstairs. There was even a pet _____ to help the guests find their way to the dance hall. You see, he could see in the dark, and since the castle was poorly lit, he was the only one who could find the way easily. There was even a _____ for people to pet, to make them feel at home. There were so many twists and turns going up the stairs, people almost needed a _____ to find their way. When they finally got to the main room, _____ was there waiting to shake everybody's _____. There was food, music, and fun— all the ingredients for a great party!

RULE #2: DO THE BEST YOU CAN DO
with Long "A"

> *Hi! My name is Wavy Davy. I've waited all day to tell you about the long "a." Just say the name of the letter "a." That's it! The long "a." Hurray! Okay. It's also my birthday today. Sing along to this song and wish me a happy birthday!*

I. Breaking the Ice Sure Feels Nice

BIRTHDAY

<u>Chorus:</u>
You say it's your birthday
It's my birthday too, yeah
You say it's your birthday
We're gonna* have a good time.
I'm glad it's your birthday
Happy birthday to you

*gonna=going to

**goin'=going

Yes, we're gonna have a party, party
Yes, we're goin'** to a party, party
Yes, we're goin' to a party, party
Yes, we're goin' to a party, party
I would like you to dance   Birthday
Now, take a cha-cha-cha-chance   Birthday
I would like you to dance   Birthday
Dance!

II. Read, Read! Yes, Indeed!

Hey! I got a letter from Davy in the mail about his birthday. What a crazy way to spend the day!

Dear Nan,

Today, my Mom baked a cake. It was

fate. My Dad said, "This tastes

great!" It was first rate. Then we

played a game 'cause outside the

rain was falling. So, to keep

from straining my brain,

L
O
N
G

A

we played a board game. But it was

lame. So I went to get the mail. The

rain had turned to hail! I stumbled on

a nail. Across the street was a

garage sale. They were selling a

cape, a safe, and a table. I paid $8

for the table. You should've seen my

father's face! He hated it!

III. I Can't Wait for My Birth Date

What's your birthday? What month? What day? What year? Tell a friend.

January

February

March

What are the months of the year?

April

May

June

July

August

September

October

November

December

Who was born this month? Let's sing them "Happy Birthday"!

IV. Sing Along to My Song

I'm Fraidy Freddy, and I'm afraid of a lot of things. But, I LOVE ONIONS. Can you smell them on my breath? Circle all the words containing the long "a" vowel sound.

L O N G A

I LOVE ONIONS

I don't like snails or toads or frogs
Or strange things living under logs
But ummm. I love onions.
I don't like dancin' with crazy teddys
Always jumpin' on my head
But ummm. I love onions.

Chorus x 2
Onions. Onions. La La La
Onions. Onions. Ha Ha Ha
Root toot toot doot Toot toot doot

I don't like rain or snow or hail
Or Moby Dick, the great white whale
But ummm. I love onions.
I don't like shoes that pinch your toes
Or people who squirt you with the
    garden hose
But ummm. I love onions.

[Chorus] x 2

An onion is a tuberous vegetable
And is a member of the genus
    stinkus delicioso
It was highly prized by the
    ancient Egyptian Pharos and
    their friends and cousins.
It causes watering of the eyes
    and rubifaction of the skin,
    but it is very very tasty.

[Chorus] x 2

How very very crude.

V.   Use Your Brain to Explain

I'm Zaney Paint. What are the things you love or hate in "I Love Onions" with the long "a" vowel sound? Draw them in the spaces below, or paint them if you like.

VI.   Your Turn—What Did You Learn?

THINGS YOU LIKE:

1.   _____

2.   _____

3.   _____

4.   _____

5.   _____

THINGS YOU DON'T LIKE:

1.   _____

2.   _____

3.   _____

4.   _____

5.   _____

Let's make a list of the things we like and don't like using nouns. Then, we're going to create new words to "I Love Onions." After you finish your lists, let's sing our new songs to the class!

I LOVE _____

I don't like _____ or _____
   or frogs
Or strange things living under logs
But ummm. I love _____
I don't like dancin' with
   crazy _____
Always jumpin' on my _____
But ummm. I love _____.

Chorus

_____. _____. La La La
_____. _____. Ha Ha Ha
Root toot toot doot Toot toot doot

RULE #3: DREAM BIG DREAMS
with Short "E"

I. Breakin' the Ice Sure Feels Nice

Hi! I'm Henry! The short "e" vowel sounds like someone pushed you gently in the stomach. It's in my name —Henry. By the way, I just got married. I wrote a song about myself you might enjoy!

I'M HENRY VIII, I AM

I'm Henry the eighth I am

Henry the eighth I am, I am.

I got married to the widow next door

She's been married seven times before

And every one was a Henry (Henry)

She wouldn't have a Willy or a Sam

(or a Sam!)

I'm her eighth old man, I'm Henry

Henry the eighth I am

Second verse same as the first.

HENRY I

HENRY II

I'm Henry the eighth I am

Henry the eighth I am, I am.

I got married to the widow next door

She's been married seven times before

And every one was a Henry (Henry)

She wouldn't have a Willy or a Sam

                  (or a Sam!)

I'm her eighth old man, I'm Henry

Henry the eighth I am, I am

Henry the eighth I am.

HENRY III

HENRY IV

HENRY V

HENRY VI

HENRY VII

HENRY VIII

II. What Does It Mean, Jelly Bean?

Hi! I'm Wendy Red. They call me "Red" because I'm a redhead.

I have it in my head that it's time for

me **to wed**. It's something my

mother **said**, and something that I

read. And you can guess, I'll be a

mess until I'm married. I **confess**.

You can bet, I'm ready to get set with

my lovely pet. So, I**'m sending** you

an invitation **to attend**. I **beg** you to

let me **jet** you to the reception so you

can be well **fed**. Please be my guest.

Please, say "YES."

III. HAMMER THE GRAMMAR

Examine Wendy's essay. Some of the words are underlined. Can you guess why? List them below. After you've listed them, look them up in the dictionary. What do they all have in common?

What is a verb? It's the part of speech that tells you what action happened. The noun tells "who," and the verb tells "what."

1. _____

2. _____

3. _____

4. _____

5. _____

6. _____

7. _____

8. _____

9. _____

IV. Write Your Own Tune, Man in the Moon

Remember the song, "A Ram Sam Sam" from Chapter 1? We're going to change it slightly and substitute short "e" verbs into the song.

Rhyming Dictionary					
sell	tell	check	rest	bend	pet
get	send	test	let	wreck	spell

Go _____ ____ _____

Go _____ ____ _____

Goolie Goolie Goolie
    Goolie Goolie

_____ _____ _____

RULE #4: JUST EXPLORE with Long "E"

I. Breaking the Ice Sure Feels Nice

My name is Stevie Submarine. The long "e" vowel sound is just like when you say the letter "e." It's in my name, Stevie. You know, I had the weirdest dream the other night. But before I tell you about it, I'd like to teach you a rhyme about ice cream. Do you know what to say to your parents to get them to buy you some? Try this little rhyme. Just keep saying it over and over to them until they give in, ok?

I'd like to tell you about my dream now. I even wrote a song called "Octopus's Garden" about the dream. My song sounds a lot like the Beatles' song. See if it is as strange to you as it is to me.

I scream. You scream.

We all scream for ice cream.

OCTOPUS'S GARDEN

Verse #1

I'd like to be under the sea
In an octopus's garden in the shade.
He'd let us in—knows where we've been
In his octopus's garden in the shade.
I'd ask my friends to come and see
An octopus's garden with me.
I'd like to be under the sea
In an octopus's garden in the shade.

Verse #2

We would be warm below the storm
In our little hideaway* beneath the waves
Resting our head on the sea bed
In an octopus's garden near a cave
We would sing and dance around
Because we know we can't be found
I'd like to be under the sea
In an octopus's garden in the shade.

*hideaway=hiding place

Verse #3

We would shout and swim about
The coral that lies beneath the waves
Oh what joy for every girl and boy
Knowing that they're happy
  and they're safe
We would be so happy you and me
No one there to tell us what to do
I'd like to be under the sea
In an octopus's garden with you.
In an octopus's garden with you.
In an octopus's garden with you.

II. What Do You Hear? Is It Clear?

Which words in "Octopus's Garden" contain the short "e" vowel sound? List them below.

Which words in the song contain the long "e" vowel sound? List them here.

Long E:

1. _____
2. _____
3. _____
4. _____
5. _____
6. _____
7. _____
8. _____

Short E:

1. _____
2. _____
3. _____
4. _____
5. _____
6. _____
7. _____

L
O
N
G

E

III. HAMMER THE GRAMMAR

Find the verbs in "Octopus's Garden" which are coupled with the helping verb "would."

Verbs + Helping Verb "Would":

1. _____
2. _____
3. _____
4. _____
5. _____
6. _____

IV. Your Turn—What Did You Learn?

Stevie wrote an essay about what he believes. Read what he wrote and put a circle around all the nouns with long "e" and put a square around all the verbs with long "e."

I believe in being free in the sea. I seek to feel complete, feeding the eels green seaweed and orange peels. I sleep in my jeep and then leap into the deep. I weep with joy and wipe my cheek because it's so sweet. It's a treat to be me.

RULE #5: Do What Makes You Feel Alive with Short "I"

I. Breakin' the Ice Sure Feels Nice

Have you ever had the hiccups? You know the sound you make when you're hiccupping? Well, that's the short "i" vowel sound, like in this little song.

A TISKET A TASKET*

A tisket, a tasket
A green and yellow basket
I took my treasure to the school
And on the way I dropped it!

A tisket, a tasket
A green and yellow basket
I took my treasure to the school
And on the way I lost it!

See the big letters? That's where you can hear the short "i." Can you hear it? Try hiccupping before you sing it. Now can you hear it?

*tisket, a tasket=
nonsense words

II. What Does It Mean, Jelly Bean?

My name is Hip Zip. I'm not **rich**, and

I'm not **sick**. But I am **thin**.

My outfit is a **big** hit even if it

is **slinky**. I'm **cool**.

I'm **slick**. My fashion

ideas are going to stick.

Examine Hip Zip's essay. Some of the words are underlined. Can you guess why? List them below. After you've listed them, look them up in the dictionary. What do they all have in common?

1. _____ 5. _____

2. _____ 6. _____

3. _____ 7. _____

4. _____

What is an adjective? It's the part of speech that describes something or someone. We use adjectives to describe nouns.

III. Movin' and Groovin'

Listen to "Itsy Bitsy Teenie Weenie Yellow Polkadot Bikini" and dance, dance, dance.

ITSY BITSY TEENIE WEENIE YELLOW POLKA-DOT BIKINI

Verse #1

She was afraid to come out of the locker

She was as nervous as she could be

She was afraid to come out of the locker

She was afraid that somebody would see

(Two, three, four, tell the people what she wore)

Chorus

It was an itsy bitsy teenie weenie yellow polkadot bikini

That she wore for the first time today

An itsy bitsy teenie weenie yellow polkadot bikini

+++So in the locker she wanted to stay

(Two, three, four, stick around we'll tell ya more)

[+++ This line changes for each chorus.]

Verse #2

She was afraid to come out in the open

And so a blanket around her she wore

She was afraid to come out in the open

And so she sat bundled up* on the shore

(Two, three, four, tell the people what she wore)

Chorus [modified]

+++So in the blanket she wanted to stay

Verse #3

Now she's afraid to come out of the water

And I wonder what she's going to do

Now she's afraid to come out of the water

And the poor little girl's turning blue**

(Two, three, four, tell the people what she wore)

Chorus [modified]

+++So in the water she wanted to stay

*bundled up=wrapped up

**turning blue=she was getting so cold, she was turning blue

IV. HAMMER THE GRAMMAR

Find the adjectives in "Itsy Bitsy Teenie Weenie Yellow Polkadot Bikini." Remember, adjectives are words that describe someone or something.

1. _____

2. _____

3. _____

4. _____

5. _____

6. _____

7. _____

8. _____

9. _____

10. _____

11. _____

Can you solve the crossword puzzle by finding synonyms for the words? Synonyms* are words that mean the same thing.

Down

1. Wavy Davy is glad. What is another word for glad?

3. Stevie Submarine is nice to people. What's another word for someone who is nice to people?

5. Wendy Red is anxious about finding a husband. Is there another word for anxious?

Across

2. Fraidy Freddy is frightened. What is another word for this?

4. Madelyn is mad. What's another word for mad?

6. Hip Zip is beautiful. Is there another word for this?

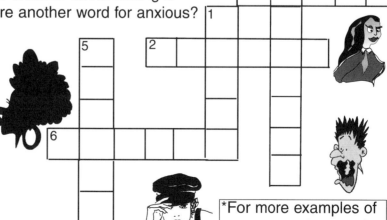

*For more examples of synonyms, please refer to page 93.

SHORT I

V.   Your Turn—What Did You Learn?

Describe the person sitting next to you by making a list of adjectives that describe him or her.

ADJECTIVES:

1. _____

2. _____

3. _____

4. _____

5. _____

Can you find synonyms for these adjectives? Check on page 93 to see if we have some synonyms ready for you. If not, what would you do? That's right! You would look the words up in a **thesaurus**. A thesaurus is for finding synonyms and antonyms.

SYNONYMS:

1. _____

2. _____

3. _____

4. _____

5. _____

RULE #6: DOING WHAT YOU LOVE STICKS
with Long "I"

I. Read, Read! Yes, Indeed!

Hi! My name is Tiny Wylie. The long "i" vowel sound is just like saying the name of the letter "i." It's also in my name: Tiny Wylie. By the way, I like to write. Why don't you read my essay and tell me what you think?

They call me **tiny**, but I'm not. I eat

all the time, **spicy** food of any kind.

High calorie is just **fine**—nothing

light. And I can eat all night. Ice

cream is **nice**. I also like **fried** rice.

I even like to eat it twice. My favorite

drink is Slice. I like my Slice with ice

at the **right** price. Sometimes, I like

Salsa. I like it **hot**, not **mild**. That's

my style. Give me an inch and I'll

take a mile.

II. Write Your Own Tune, Man in the Moon

Rhyming Dictionary			
kind	ripe	white	nice
fine	light	bright	right

Remember the song, "A Ram Sam Sam" from Chapter 1? We're going to change it slightly and substitute long "i" adjectives into the song.

So _____ _____ _____
So _____ _____ _____
Goolie Goolie Goolie
    Goolie Goolie
_____ _____ _____

III. Sing Along to My Song

LONG I

CHICKEN LIPS AND LIZARD HIPS

Verse #1
When I was just a little kid, I never liked to eat
And Mama would put things on my plate
  and I'd dump 'em* on her feet
But then one day
  she made this soup—
  And I ate it all in bed
I asked her what she put in it and well,
this is what she said

*em = them

I'm not like Wylie. I don't like to eat very much. My Mom used to make me eat a soup she made called "Mama's Soup Surprise." I wrote a song about it. Sing along with me!

Chorus

Chicken lips and lizard hips
  and alligator eyes
Monkey legs
  and buzzard eggs and
  salamander thighs
Rabbit ears and camel rears
  and tasty toenail pies
Stir 'em all together and
It's Mama's Soup Surprise

Verse #2

Well, I went into the bathroom
  And I stood beside the sink
I said, "I'm feelin' slightly ill,
  And I think I'd like a drink.
Mama said, "I've just the thing
  I'll get it in a wink**.
It's full of lots of protein
  And vitamins I think!"

**in a
wink=immediately

<u>Chorus</u>

Well, chicken lips and lizard hips
   and alligator eyes
Monkey legs
   and buzzard eggs and
   salamander thighs
Rabbit ears and camel rears
   and tasty toenail pies
Stir 'em all together and
It's Mama's Soup Surprise
Mama's Soup Surprise!

Just to make sure you're hearing the long "i" vowel sound, review the lyrics to "Chicken Lips and Lizard Hips" and circle all the long "i" words. Let's review some grammar, too. Put a square around all the adjectives you find.

L O N G I

IV. ANTONYMS DESCRIBING THINGS

How are Hip Zip and Tiny Wylie different? We've read both of their essays and we've learned a lot about them. What do you think? In our Dictionary are some "antonyms." Antonyms are words that mean the opposite of each other. Make a list for Hip Zip and then make a list for Tiny Wylie. Use our Dictionary list if you need ideas. For more detailed information on antonyms, please refer to page 94.

Hip Zip is:

1. _____
2. _____
3. _____
4. _____
5. _____
6. _____
7. _____
8. _____

ANTONYMS = DIFFERENT

Tiny Wylie is:

1. _____
2. _____
3. _____
4. _____
5. _____
6. _____
7. _____
8. _____

DICTIONARY

Tall
Ugly
Thin
Boring
Unhealthy
Young
Full
Friendly
Big
Sick
Cool
Rich
Happy
Male
Nice
Generous
Kind

V. Your Turn—What Did You Learn?

Now it's your turn to write a paragraph in which you describe someone or something. Remember, adjectives will help you. You can use synonyms and antonyms, too. Why don't you tell me something about YOU. I'd like to get to know you better.

_____

_____

_____

_____

_____

_____

RULE #7: Use What You've Been Given
with Short "O"

I. Breakin' the Ice Sure Feels Nice

What do you say when someone's dinner falls on the floor and they were really hungry? Or when the doctor wants to see if you have a sore throat, and he puts the tongue depresser in your mouth, remember what you say? It's probably something like the short "o" vowel.

<u>On Top Of Spaghetti</u>

On top of spaghetti all covered with cheese,

I lost my poor meatball when somebody sneezed.

It rolled off the table and onto the floor,

And then my poor meatball rolled out of the door.

It rolled in the garden and under a bush,

And then my poor meatball was nothing but mush.

The mush was as tasty as tasty could be,

And early last summer it grew into a tree.

The tree was all covered with beautiful moss.

It grew great big meatballs and tomato sauce.

So if you eat spaghetti all covered with cheese,

Hold on to your meatball and don't ever sneeze.

When did most of the story in "On Top of Spaghetti" happen? Was it yesterday or last summer? We can't be sure, but at least we know it happened in the past. How do we write a regular verb in the past tense? That's it! We add "ed" to the end. And sometimes, verbs in the past tense are irregular or unusual.* If you can, write the regular and irregular past tense verbs from "On Top of Spaghetti" in the list below.

*For a list of 100 common irregular verbs, please refer to pages 95-98.

1. _____   4. _____

2. _____   5. _____

3. _____   6. _____

II. Read, Read! Yes, Indeed!

Hi! My name is Bobbie Socks. I wrote something in my diary the other day. Why not read it? If you have any thoughts, let me know!

S
H
O
R
T
O

I think a **<u>lot</u>** about what I've been

taught. I need to arrive right on the

dot. I live by the clock. America is an

on-time online kind of grind. We act

oddly. In fact, we go bonkers trying

not to be late. We run; we don't walk.

We give it everything we've got. We

don't work **sloppily**. Oh no! We don't

yacht **choppily**. Oh no! Instead, we're

Johnny on the spot!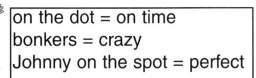

on the dot = on time
bonkers = crazy
Johnny on the spot = perfect

III. HAMMER THE GRAMMAR

Some of the words in Bobbie's diary entry are underlined. Can you figure out why? After you've listed them down below, look them up in your dictionary. What do they all have in common?

1. _____

2. _____

3. _____

4. _____

5. _____

*What is an adverb? It's the part of speech that tells you **how** the action happened. The noun tells "who," the verb tells "what," the adjective describes the nouns and the adverbs describe the verbs!*

IV. Movin' and Groovin'

This is a rockin' be-boppin' song. Sing along! Right on! After you've listened to the song, review the lyrics. Circle all the words you find with the short "o" vowel sound.

S H O R T O

(We're Gonna) Rock Around the Clock

Verse #1

One, two, three o'clock, four o'clock rock

Five, six, seven o'clock, eight o'clock rock

Nine, ten, eleven o'clock, twelve o'clock rock

We're gonna rock around the clock tonight

Verse #2

Put your glad rags* on,
Join me Hon
We'll have some fun
  when the clock strikes one
We're gonna rock around
  the clock tonight
We're gonna rock, rock, rock,
  'til broad daylight
Gonna rock, gonna rock
  around the clock tonight

*glad rags = party clothes

Verse #3

When the clock strikes two,
  three and four
If the band slows down
  we'll yell for more
We're gonna rock around
  the clock tonight
We're gonna rock, rock, rock,
  'til broad daylight
Gonna rock, gonna rock
  around the clock tonight
[Instrumental]

Verse #4

When the chimes ring five,
  six, and seven
We'll be right in seventh heaven*
We're gonna rock
  around the clock tonight
We're gonna rock, rock, rock,
  'til broad daylight
Gonna rock, gonna rock
  around the clock tonight

Verse #5

When it's eight, nine, ten, eleven too
I'll be goin' strong and so will you
We're gonna rock
  around the clock tonight
We're gonna rock, rock, rock,
  'til broad daylight
Gonna rock, gonna rock
  around the clock tonight

Verse #6

When the clock strikes twelve
  we'll cool off** then
Start rockin' 'round
  the clock again
We're gonna rock
  around the clock tonight
We're gonna rock, rock, rock,
  'til broad daylight
Gonna rock, gonna rock
  around the clock tonight

*seventh heaven =
highest level of heaven

**cool off = relax

V. Your Turn—What Did You Learn?

What verb tense is most common in "Rock Around the Clock"? Mostly this song is in the future or implies the future. How do we make a verb express the future? We add a helping verb, "will," to the main verb. Sometimes "will" is abbreviated like this: "'ll" as in "we'll." Also, the phrase "we're gonna" or "we're going to" means something is planned in the future.

Go back and study the lyrics to "Rock Around the Clock." Put a square around all instances of "will" and "gonna." How many did you find?

RULE #8: Feel Free to Create with Long "O"

I. Breaking the Ice Sure Feels Nice

Hi! My name is Lonely Codie. I'm lonely because my girlfriend left me the other day. I wrote this song about it. I've been listening to a lot of Led Zeppelin, so it sounds like one of their songs. Anyway, it would make me feel better if you would sing along with me. Thanks. By the way, the long "o" vowel sounds like the name of the letter "o." Do me a favor and circle all the words in my song that have this sound.

Chorus
Oh oh oh oh oh
You don't have to go—
oh oh oh oh
You don't have to go—
oh oh oh oh
You don't have to go!

Ay Ay Ay Ay Ay
All those tears I cry ay ay ay ay
All those tears I cry oh oh oh oh
Baby, please don't go!

When I read the letter
  that you wrote me
It made me mad mad mad
When I read the words
  that it told me
It made me sad sad sad
But I still love you so
I can't let you go
I love you
Oh, baby I love you oh!

[Chorus Repeated]

L
O
N
G

O

II. Making Sense of Verb Tense

Present:

1. _____
2. _____
3. _____
4. _____
5. _____

When do we use present tense? We use present tense when something happens routinely or habitually. Codie's song contains present tense verbs and irregular past tense verbs. List below all the verbs in the present tense and in the second list, write verbs you think might be past tense irregular verbs. You can always use pages 95-98 to check irregular verb tenses!

Past:

1. _____
2. _____
3. _____
4. _____

III. Sing! Sing! Let Your Voice Ring!

Hi! I'm Holy Moley. I don't like doctors very much, but the other day my sister had a stomachache and she had to go to the doctor. I wrote a song about it. By the way, the long "o" is just saying the name of the letter "o," like in my name: Holy Moley.

Coconut

Verse #1

Brother bought a coconut; he bought it for a dime.
His sister had another one. She paid it for the lime.
She put the lime in the coconut. She drank 'em both up
She put the lime in the coconut. She drank 'em both up

Verse #1 (continued)

She put the lime in the coconut.
She drank 'em both up
She put the lime in the coconut.
She called the doctor
   and woke him up.

She said, "Doctor, ain't there nothin' I can take?"
She said, "Doctor, to relieve this belly ache,"
She said, "Doctor, ain't there nothin' I can take?"
She said, "Doctor, to relieve this belly ache?"

Verse #2

He said, "Now, let me get this straight.*
You put the lime in the coconut.
You drank 'em both up.
You put the lime in the coconut.
You drank 'em both up.
You put the lime in the coconut.
You drank 'em both up.
You put the lime in the coconut.
You called your doctor
   and woke him up."

*Let me get this straight = Let me try to understand this.

LONG O

Verse #2 (continued)

You said, "Doctor, ain't there nothin' I can take?"
You said, "Doctor,
    to relieve this belly ache,"
You said, "Doctor,
    ain't there nothin' I can take?"
You said, "Doctor, to relieve this belly ache?"

Verse #3

"You put the lime in the coconut.
You drink 'em both together.
You put the lime in the coconut,
And you'll feel better.
Put the lime in the coconut
And drink 'em both up
Put the lime in the coconut
And call me in the morning.
Yes, you call me in the morning.
If you call me in the morning,
    I'll tell you what to do.
If you call me in the morning,
    I'll tell you what to do.
If you call me in the morning,
    I'll tell you what to do.

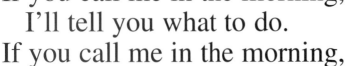

"Coconut" contains present, past, and future tense verbs. Please underline the present tense verbs you find. Put a square around the past tense verbs, and circle any future tense verbs you find.

IV. Read, Read! Yes, Indeed!

I wrote a story about the doctor, too. Why don't you read it?

I feel like a ghost. My bones hurt. I

called the doctor on the phone. I told

her jokingly that I couldn't cope. She

said coldly, "Don't drink coke." I

replied, "I only drink rootbeer floats."

L
O
N
G

O

Boldly, I broke into a smile and said, "I

only soak in Coke when I'm at the end

of my rope. Hopefully, I'll no longer

feel lonely." My doctor laughed.

V. Your Turn—What Did You Learn?

To make sure you understand verb tenses and adverbs, please examine Codey's story again. Underline all the present tense verbs. Circle all the past tense verbs. Put a square around all of the adverbs. Finally, put a triangle around all of the long "o" words.

RULE #9: Use More Than Your Mind with Short "U"

I. Breakin' the Ice Sure Feels Nice

<u>A Hundred Ten Bottles of Milk</u>

A hundred three bottles of milk on the wall

A hundred three bottles of milk

You take one down and pass it around

A hundred two bottles of milk on the wall

A hundred two bottles of milk on the wall

A hundred two bottles of milk

You take one down and pass it around

A hundred one bottles of milk on the wall

[Repeat with one hundred one, one

hundred, and finally ninety-nine]

Have you ever not understood someone and said "huh"? It's not very polite, but we do it sometimes. That vowel sound in "huh" is the short "u" vowel sound, like the vowel sound in "hundred" in this little song.

Americans sing this song when we're taking long car trips and we're bored. This is a fun way to pass the time. Just keep subtracting bottles of milk until you get to zero. It'll drive your parents crazy!

S
H
O
R
T
U

II. Movin' and Groovin'

My girlfriend left me. I have a lot of time to think now. So, I wrote this song. It sounds just like Del Shannon's song from the 1960's, but I still like it. Just for fun, see if you can hear the short "u" vowel sound. Circle all the words with the short "u." It'll cheer me up.

RUNAWAY

Verse #1

As I walk along I wonder
   what went wrong with our love,
   a love that was so strong
And as I still walk on I think of
   the things we've done together,
   while our hearts were young

Chorus

I'm a-walkin' in the rain
Tears are fallin' and
   I feel the pain
Wishin' you were here by me
To end this misery
And I wonder
I wa-wa-wa-wa-wonder
Why? Why-why-why-why-why
   she ran away and I wonder
   where she will stay
My little runaway,
   run–run-run-run-runaway

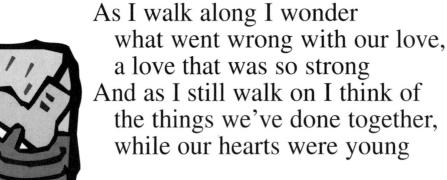

Chorus [Repeat]

I'm a-walkin' in the rain
Tears are fallin' and I feel the pain
Wishin' you were here by me
To end this misery
And I wonder
I wa-wa-wa-wa-wonder
Why…Why-why-why-why-why
  she ran away
And I wonder where she will stay
My little runaway,
    run–run-run-run-runaway
    run–run-run-run-runaway

III. HAMMER THE GRAMMAR

*Today we're going to look at pronouns. Pronouns have different functions. When they replace a noun and they come **before** the verb, they're called "subject pronouns." Look at the chart to the right. Then put a square around all the subject pronouns in "Runaway."*

Sometimes pronouns show that something belongs to someone or possession. We call these pronouns possessive adjectives. Put a triangle around all of the possessive adjectives in "Runaway.

Subject Pronouns
I
You
He
She
It
We
They

Possessive Adjectives	
My	Our
Your	Its
His	Their
Her	

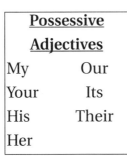

Present Progressive:

1. ———————
———————
2. ———————
———————

There is another verb tense called the progressive verb form. It is made of the verb "to be" plus "i-n-g." Say that for me: "The verb 'to be' plus 'i-n-g.'" That's a rhyme and makes it easy to remember. The present progressive looks like this: "I am eating." Look at "Runaway" and see if you can find any instances of the present progressive.

IV. Read, Read! Yes, Indeed!

Hello. My name is Sunny Nunn. My boyfriend left me and so now I don't have anyone. But I can't stop thinking about him. So, I wrote this little paragraph. Would you mind reading it and underlining all the words with the short "u"?

I once was in love with someone. I was so lucky. He was a nut, but I loved him. He drove a truck. He loved the sun and having fun. That's why he was my number one.

RULE #10: Learning Is Your Friend with Long "U"

I. Write Your Own Tune, Man in the Moon

The long "u" vowel is simply saying the name of the letter: "u."

Remember the song, "A Ram Sam Sam" from Chapter 1? We're going to change it slightly and substitute long "u" words into the song as well as new possessive adjectives for each time through.

Rhyming Dictionary

broom	mew	soup	flute	loop	tune

Possessive Adjectives	
My	Our
Your	Its
His	Their
Her	

My _____ _____ _____

My _____ _____ _____

Goolie Goolie Goolie
Goolie Goolie

_____ _____ _____

LONG U

Howdy! My name is Rudy. I'm not sad! I'm in LOVE! Oooooh wheee! The vowel sound in my name, Rudy, is the long "u." I'm even in love with the sound of the long "u" vowel. I have never been so happy! I wrote a song. Come on! Sing along to my song!

II. Breakin' the Ice Sure Feels Nice

TUTTI FRUTTI

A Womp Bomp a loo ah, a lop bam boom

[CHORUS]
Tutti Frutti, oh rootie
Tutti Frutti, whooo!
Tutti Frutti, oh rootie
Tutti Frutti, oh rootie
Tutti Frutti, oh rootie
A Womp Bomp a loo ah, a lop bam boom

SUE

I got a gal named Sue.
She knows how to be true
I got a gal named Sue.
She knows how to be true
I've been to the east.
I've been to the west,
But she's the gal that I love the best
[CHORUS]

Object Pronouns
Me
You
Him
Her
It
Us
Them

I got a gal named Daisy
She almost drives me crazy
I got a gal named Daisy
She almost drives me crazy
She knows how to trust me, yes indeed
Boy, don't you know
   she's going with me!

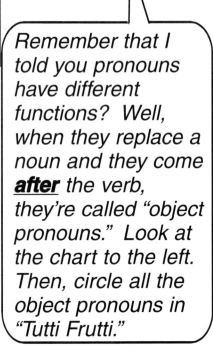
DAISY

*Remember that I told you pronouns have different functions? Well, when they replace a noun and they come **after** the verb, they're called "object pronouns." Look at the chart to the left. Then, circle all the object pronouns in "Tutti Frutti."*

[CHORUS]

III. What Does It Mean, Jelly Bean?

Rudy loves Sue: her boots, her stew, her cute moods. And Sue loves Rudy: his loot, his dune buggy, his attitude. It makes me want to puke. Why can't Sue find someone new?

My name is Lucy. I'm choosy about my friends. I don't like just anyone. And right now, I'm disappointed in my friend Sue. She likes Rudy. And he's so goofy!

L O N G

U

IV. Sing! Sing! Let Your Voice Ring!

Hi! I'm Suzy Que. I'm the one who loves Rudy! Isn't he cute? My grandmother taught me a song that's perfect for Rudy and me. I sing it to him every chance I get. Do you want to learn a lovely tune to sing to your sweetiepoo?

By the Light of the Silvery Moon

By the light of the silvery moon
I want to spoon.
To my honey I'll croon loves tune
Honey moon, keep a shinin' in June
Your silvery beams will bring love's dreams
We'll be cuddlin' soon by the silvery moon

[Repeat]

V. Your Turn—What Did You Learn?

To see if you can hear the short "u" and the long "u" vowel sound, please examine the lyrics to "By the Light of the Silvery Moon." List the words that contain these vowel sounds in the spaces provided below.

Short u:

1. _____
2. _____
3. _____
4. _____

Long u:

1. _____
2. _____
3. _____
4. _____
5. _____
6. _____

Pronoun   Type

_____   _____

_____   _____

_____   _____

_____   _____

In this Chapter, we've also been studying subject pronouns, object pronouns, and possessive adjectives. Can you find any of these in "By the Light of the Silvery Moon"? List the pronoun, and beside your choice, list what type it is.

L
O
N
G

U

RULE #11: Keep the Learning Pleasant with Short "oo" and Diphthong "oy"

I. Breaking the Ice Sure Feels Nice

Who Stole the Cookies?

Hello! I'm Brook. I love eating cookies. The bad part is that they stick to my thighs! Anyway, I wanted to tell you that the short "oo" vowel sound is strange. Listen carefully to the word "cookies" in this fun little song.

Who stole the cookies from the cookie jar?
Who stole the cookies from the cookie jar?
Who stole the cookies from the cookie jar?
Johnny stole the cookies from the cookie jar!
Who me? Yes, you!
Couldn't be! Then who?
Who stole the cookies from the cookie jar?
Who stole the cookies from the cookie jar?
Who stole the cookies from the cookie jar?
Freddy stole the cookies from the cookie jar!
Who me? Yes, you!
Couldn't be! Then who?
Who stole the cookies from the cookie jar?
Who stole the cookies from the cookie jar?
Who stole the cookies from the cookie jar?
Dad stole the cookies from the cookie jar!
Who me? Yes, you!
Well, actually it was me. I was kind of hungry, and I was hoping you might have some more!

II. What Does It Mean, Jelly Bean?

Hi! My name is Rooky Crook. Look at what I wrote in my private book! I love to write and I think it's pretty good! All of the underlined words have the short "oo." Can you hear it?

I love reading a **good book**. It took

me all day to read about Captain

Hook. I love fishing, too. I **shook** the

worm, put it on my **hook**, and then put

on my **hood**. Fish tastes **good**! My

mother has never **understood** how I

could hook a fish. She doesn't think

that I **should**. Hey! I want to **look**

good. With a last name like, "**Crook**,"

I've done all that I **could**. I even **cook**

from a **cookbook**!

III. Movin' and Groovin'

> I met this guy when I was in the Army. He played the trumpet! He loved playing the trumpet more than anything else in the whole world. My girlfriends and I wrote this song about him. It has a lot of the short "oo" vowel sound in it **and** it's fun to sing!

Boogie Woogie Bugle Boy

Verse #1

He was a famous trumpet man
   from out Chicago way
He had a boogie style that no one
   else could play
He was the top man at his craft
But then his number came up and
   he was gone with the draft
He's in the army now, a-blowin' reveille
He's the boogie woogie bugle boy
   of Company B

Verse #2

They made him blow a bugle
   for his Uncle Sam
It really brought him down
   because he could not jam
The captain seemed to understand
Because the next day the cap'
   went out and drafted a band
And now the company jumps
   when he plays reveille
He's the boogie woogie bugle boy
   of Company B

Verse #3

A-root, a-toot,
  a-toot-diddelyada-toot
He blows it eight-to-the-bar,
  in boogie rhythm

He can't blow a note
  unless the bass
  and guitar are
  playin' with him
And the company jumps
  when he plays
  reveille

He's the boogie woogie
  bugle boy of
  Company B

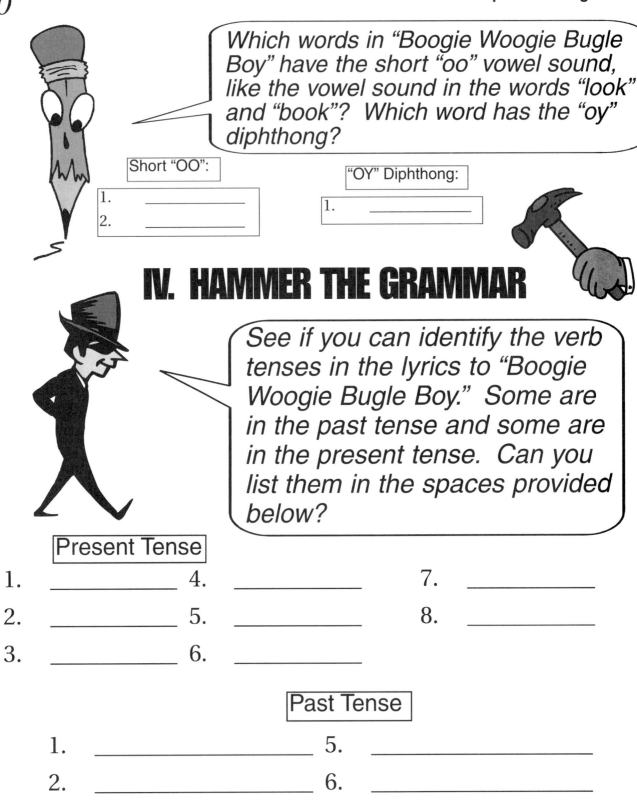

Which words in "Boogie Woogie Bugle Boy" have the short "oo" vowel sound, like the vowel sound in the words "look" and "book"? Which word has the "oy" diphthong?

Short "OO":

1. _____
2. _____

"OY" Diphthong:

1. _____

IV. HAMMER THE GRAMMAR

See if you can identify the verb tenses in the lyrics to "Boogie Woogie Bugle Boy." Some are in the past tense and some are in the present tense. Can you list them in the spaces provided below?

Present Tense

1. _____   4. _____   7. _____
2. _____   5. _____   8. _____
3. _____   6. _____

Past Tense

1. _____   5. _____
2. _____   6. _____
3. _____   7. _____
4. _____   8. _____

V. Sing Along to My Song

WOOLY BULLY

I went to a dance the other night and I overheard a conversation. I love to listen to other people talk to each other. So, I decided to write about it. It sounds exactly like Domingo Samudio's song, but I guess we both experienced the exact same thing!

Matty told Hatty about a thing she saw
Had two big horns and a wooly jaw
Wooly bully, wooly bully.
Wooly bully, wooly bully, wooly bully.
Well, Hatty told Matty,
    "Let's don't take no chance.
    Let's not be L-seven,*
    Come on and learn to dance.
Wooly bully, wooly bully.
Wooly bully, wooly bully, wooly bully.
[Instrumental]
Matty told Hatty,
    "That's the thing to do.
    Get you someone really
    To pull the wool with you."
Wooly bully, wooly bully.
Wooly bully, wooly bully, wooly bully.

*L-seven = conservative

VI. Your Turn—What Did You Learn?

Can you pick out the short "oo" vowel words in "Wooly Bully"?

1. _____   3. _____

2. _____   4. _____

RULE #12: The Rhythm's In Yourself with "ow/ou" and Control-R Vowels

I. Breakin' the Ice Sure Feels Nice

Surfin' Bird

Hi! I'm loudmouth Burt! I love to surf. I have a talent for surfing. So, my friends call me the "Surfing Bird" or just "Bird" for short. They even wrote me a song. Could you sing it to me?

A-well a everybody's heard about the bird

B-b-b-bird, bird, b-bird's the word

A-well-a bird, bird, bird, the bird is the word

A-well-a bird, bird, bird,
　well the bird is the word

A-well-a bird, bird, bird, b-bird's the word

A-well-a bird, bird, bird,
　well the bird is the word

A-well-a bird, bird, b-bird's the word

A-well-a bird, bird, bird,
　b-bird's the word

A-well-a bird, bird, bird,
　well the bird is the word

A-well a bird, bird, b-bird's the word

Well-a don't you know about the bird?

Well, everybody knows
　that the bird is the word!

A -well-a bird, bird, b-bird's the word

[REPEAT]

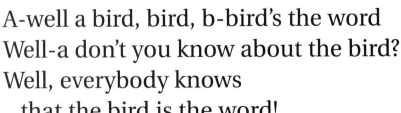

C
N
T
R
L
R

Papa-oo-mow-mow, papa-ooma-mow-mow
Papa-oo-mow-mow, papa-ooma-mow-mow
Papa-oo-mow-mow, papa-ooma-mow-mow
Papa-oo-mow-mow, papa-ooma-mow-mow
Papa-oo-mow-mow, papa-ooma-mow-mow
Papa-oo-mow-mow, papa-ooma-mow-mow
Papa-oo-mow-mow, papa-ooma-mow-mow
Papa-oo-mow-mow, papa-ooma-mow-mow
Papa-oo-mow-mow, papa-ooma-mow-mow
Papa-oo-mow-mow, papa-ooma-mow-mow
Papa-oo-mow-mow, papa-ooma-mow-mow
Papa-oo-mow-mow, papa-ooma-mow-mow
Papa-oo-mow-mow, papa-ooma-mow-mow
Papa-oo-mow-mow, papa-ooma-mow-mow
Well, don't you know about the bird?
Well, everybody knows
    that the bird is the word!
A-well-a bird, bird, b-bird's the word!

There is a sound in English that is very common. It sounds like a dog growling. Which words in "Surfin' Bird" have this growling sound?

1. _____
2. _____
3. _____

URR!

There's another sound in the second half of the "Surfin' Bird" song that sounds like the noise you make when you stub your toe or a hammer hits your thumb. What is it? That's right: "Ow!"

OW!

II. Sing Along to My Song

I am the Mighty "R" in English. I am very powerful. I can control every vowel I meet. If I come after a vowel, "a," "e," "i," "o," or "u," they don't sound the way they normally do. They are influenced by ME. I'd like to show you a song so you can see what I mean.

C
N
T
R
L

R

Swinging On A Star

Chorus:
Would you like to swing on a star
Carry moonbeams home in a jar
And be better off than you are
Or would you rather be a mule?

Verse #1:
A mule is an animal with long funny ears
He kicks up at anything he hears
His back is brawny and his brain is weak
He's just plain stupid with a stubborn streak
And by the way, if you hate to go to school
You may grow up to be a mule!

<u>Chorus</u>:
Would you like to swing on a star
Carry moonbeams home in a jar
And be better off than you are
Or would you rather be a pig?

<u>Verse #2</u>:
Hey! A pig is an animal with dirt on his face
His shoes are a terrible disgrace
He has no manners when he eats his food
He's fat and lazy and extremely rude
But if you don't care a feather or a fig
You may grow up to be a pig.

Chorus:

Would you like to swing on a star
Carry moonbeams home in a jar
And be better off than you are
Or would you rather be a fish?

Verse #3:

A fish won't do anything but swim in a brook
He can't write his name or read a book
And to fool the people is his only thought
And though he's slippery, he still gets caught
But then if that sort of life is what you wish
You may grow up to be a fish

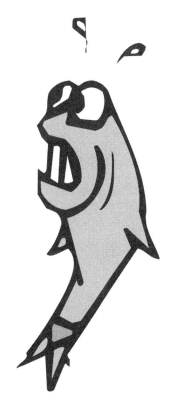

<u>Verse #4</u>:

And all the monkeys
   aren't in the zoo
Every day you meet
   quite a few
So you see it's all up to you
You can be better than you are
You could be
   swingin' on a star!

III. HAMMER THE GRAMMAR

C
N
T
R
L
R

> Examine the lyrics to "Swinging on a Star" and tell me which words the Mighty "R" is influencing. List them below.

1. _____	10. _____
2. _____	11. _____
3. _____	12. _____
4. _____	13. _____
5. _____	14. _____
6. _____	15. _____
7. _____	16. _____
8. _____	17. _____
9. _____	18. _____

> *Do you know what a helping verb is? It's the verb that helps the main verb in the sentence. One example is "should." If these helping verbs help tell you what the speaker is thinking or his "mood," they're called "modals."* See if you can find any modals in "Swinging on a Star."*

> Modals can also be used for giving advice or telling you if someone can or can't do something. There are four modals in the song. Good luck.

1. _____
2. _____
3. _____
4. _____

*For more information on modals, refer to page 99.

IV. What Does It Mean, Jelly Bean?

My name is Marge. People think I'm a little strange, so they call me "Weird Marge." I don't mind though. It's because I'm not typical. I have a lot of talents to offer to the world. The other day I wrote this about my life. What do you think?

Exercise is a great **word**. Then, I take a **shower** and feed my pet **tiger**. He's **stubborn** and **dirty**. Of course, **birds** of a

feather stick **together**! That's what I've **heard**.

V. Movin' and Groovin'

CNTRL R

Hi! I'm Kurt. I'm a roller skating nerd. Some people told me that I couldn't roller skate in their neighborhood so I wrote this song. It sounds just like the song Roger Miller sang in 1966, so it must be good.

YOU CAN'T ROLLER SKATE IN A BUFFALO HERD

Verse #1
You can't roller skate in a buffalo herd
You can't roller skate in a buffalo herd
You can't roller skate in a buffalo herd
But you can be happy if you've a mind to

You can't take a shower in a parakeet cage
You can't take a shower in a parakeet cage
You can't take a shower in a parakeet cage
But you can be happy if you've a mind to

All you've got to do is put your mind to it
Knuckle down, buckle down, do it, do it, do it

Verse #2

Well, you can't drive around
   with a tiger in your car
You can't drive around with a tiger in your car
You can't drive around with a tiger in your car
But you can be happy if you've a mind to

You can't go fishin'
   in a watermelon patch
You can't go fishin'
   in a watermelon patch
You can't go fishin'
   in a watermelon patch
But you can be happy
   if you've a mind to

All you've got to do is
   put your mind to it
Knuckle down, buckle down,
   do it, do it, do it

Well, You can't roller skate in a buffalo herd

You can't roller skate in a buffalo herd

You can't roller skate
   in a buffalo herd

But you can be happy
   if you've a mind to

Doot doot da doot doot da
   doot da doot do

Doot doot da doot doot da
   doot da doot do

Doot doot da doot doot da
   doot da doot do

But you can be happy if you've a mind to

VI. Your Turn—What Did You Learn?

To make sure you can hear Control-R words, please make a list below of all words in "You Can't Roller Skate In A Buffalo Herd" in which the vowel sound is somehow changed by the "R" that follows the vowel.

1. _____

2. _____

3. _____

4. _____

5. _____

6. _____

7. _____

8. _____

CHAPTER 13: KEEP THE BRAIN CELLS WORKING

I. LOOSEN YOUR LIPS AND MOVE YOUR HIPS

Listen to this song, "Footloose," and see if you can hear all the vowel sounds we've covered in this book.

FOOTLOOSE

Verse #1
I've been working so hard
I'm punching my card
Eight hours, for what?
Oh, tell me what I've got
I've got this feelin'
That time's just holding me down
I'll hit the ceiling
Or else I'll tear up this town

Chorus
Now I've gotta cut loose
Footloose
Kick off your Sunday shoes
Please, Louise, pull me off of my knees
Jack, get back, come on before we crack
Lose your blues—
Everybody cut footloose

Verse #2
You're playin' so cool
Obeyin' every rule
But way down in your heart
You're burnin' yearnin' for some…
Somebody to tell you
That life ain't a-passin' you by
I'm trying to tell you
It will if you don't even try!
You could fly
If you'd only cut loose!

Chorus (#2)
Footloose
Kick off your Sunday shoes
Ooh wee! Marie!
Shake it, shake it for me!
Oh, Milo—come on, come on
    let's go!
Lose your blues!
Everybody cut footloose!

Oh! Cut footloose!
Oh! Cut footloose!
Oh! Cut footloose!
You've got to turn me around
And put your feet on the ground
Now take a-hold of your soul!

Chorus (#3)
I'm turnin' it loose!
Footloose!
Kick off your Sunday shoes
Please Louise, pull me off of my knees
Jack, get back!
Come on before we crack!
Lose your blues!
Everybody cut footloose!
Everybody cut footloose!
Everybody cut footloose!
Everybody cut footloose!

II. Review Review Kalamazoo

Studying the lyrics from "Footloose," make a list of all the words that have the appropriate vowel sound under the headings below. This is a sort of test. Good luck!

Short a:	Long a:	Short e:	Long e:	Short i: (no -ing words)	Long i:
1. _____	1. _____	1. _____	1. _____	1. _____	1. _____
2. _____	2. _____	2. _____	2. _____	2. _____	2. _____
3. _____	3. _____	3. _____	3. _____	3. _____	3. _____
4. _____	4. _____	4. _____	4. _____	4. _____	4. _____
5. _____	5. _____	5. _____	5. _____	5. _____	5. _____
	6. _____	6. _____	6. _____	6. _____	6. _____
	7. _____	7. _____	7. _____	7. _____	7. _____
	8. _____	8. _____	8. _____		8. _____
			9. _____		9. _____
			10. _____		10. _____

Short o:	Long o:	Short u:	Long u:	Short oo:	ou/aw:
1. _____	1. _____	1. _____	1. _____	1. _____	1. _____
2. _____	2. _____	2. _____	2. _____	2. _____	2. _____
3. _____	3. _____	3. _____	3. _____	3. _____	3. _____
4. _____	4. _____	4. _____	4. _____		4. _____
	5. _____	5. _____	5. _____		5. _____
	6. _____	6. _____	6. _____		
	7. _____	7. _____	7. _____		
	8. _____	8. _____	8. _____		
		9. _____			
		10. _____			
		11. _____			

BOOKS /ARTICLES RECOMMENDED

*Caine, Renate Nummela, and Geoffrey Caine, <u>Making Connections</u>.
Addison-Wesley Publishing Company, Menlo Park, California, © 1991.*

*Caine, Renate Nummela, and Geoffrey Caine, <u>Education on the Edge of
Possibility</u>. Assoc. for Supervision and Curriculum Development,
Alexandria, Virginia, © 1997.*

*Campbell, Don G., <u>Introduction to the Musical Brain</u>. MMB Music, Inc.,
St. Louis, Missouri, USA, © 1983, 1992.*

*Dauer, Rebecca M., <u>Accurate English (A Complete Course in Pronunciation)</u>.
Regents/Prentice Hall, Englewood Cliffs, New Jersey, © 1993.*

*Domony, Lipz and Harris, Simpson, "Justified and Ancient: Pop Music in ESL
Classrooms," <u>ETL Journal</u>. © 1993.*

*Dryden, Gordon and Jeannette Vos, Ed.D., <u>The Learning Revolution</u>. Jalmar Press,
Rolling Hills Estates, California, USA, © 1994.*

*Freeman, Yvonne S., and David E. Freeman, <u>ESL/EFL Teaching</u>.
Heinemann Publishing, Portsmouth, New Hampshire, © 1998.*

*Jensen, Eric, <u>Music with the Brain in Mind</u>. The Brain Store, Inc.,
San Diego, California, © 2000.*

*Jensen, Eric, <u>Teaching with the Brain in Mind</u>. Assoc. for Supervision and
Curriculum Development, Alexandria, Virginia, © 1998.*

*Krashen, Stephen D. and Tracy D. Terrell, <u>The Natural Approach</u>. Alemany Press,
Regents/Prentice Hall, Englewood Cliffs, New Jersey, © 1983.*

*Kress, Jacqueline E. Ed.D., <u>The ESL Teachers' Book of Lists</u>. The Center for Applied
Research in Education, Professional Publishing, West Nyack, New York, © 1993.*

*Lazear, David, <u>Seven Ways of Teaching</u>. IRI/Skylight Training & Publishing, Inc.,
Arlington Heights, Illinois, © 1991.*

*Le Doux, J., "Emotion, Memory, and the Brain." <u>Scientific American</u>: 270, 6: 50-57,
© 1994.*

Chapters	**Phonics**	**Grammar**
Rule #1: Just Have Fun	Short A	Nouns
Rule #2: Do The Best You Can Do	Long A	Nouns
Rule #3: Dream Big Dreams	Short E	Verbs
Rule #4: Just Explore	Long E	Verbs
Rule #5: Do What Makes You Feel Alive	Short I	Adjectives, Synonyms
Rule #6: Doing What You Love Sticks	Long I	Adjectives, Antonyms

Chapters	**Phonics**	**Grammar**
Rule #7: Use What You've Been Given	Short O	Adverbs Verb Tenses
Rule #8: Feel Free To Create	Long O	Adverbs Verb Tenses
Rule #9: Use More Than Your Mind	Short U	Pronouns, Possessive Adj.
Rule #10: Learning Is Your Friend	Long U	Pronouns, Possessive Adj.
Rule #11: Keep The Learning Pleasant	Short OO Diphthong OY	Verb Tenses
Rule #12: The Rhythm's In Yourself	Diphthongs OU Control-R	Modals
Rule #13: Keep The Brain Cells Working	Review	Review Test

CHAPTER	SONG LIST
Rule #1: Just Have Fun	Rock Talk Really Rocks, A Ram Sam Sam and [Karaoke], Monster Mash
Rule #2: Do the Best You Can Do	Birthday, I Love Onions, I Love Onions [Karaoke]
Rule #3: Dream Big Dreams	I'm Henry VIII, I am, A Ram Sam Sam [Karaoke]
Rule #4: Just Explore	Octopus's Garden
Rule #5: Do What Makes You Feel Alive	A Tisket A Tasket, Itsy Bitsy Teenie Weenie Yellow Polka Dot Bikini
Rule #6: Doing What You Love Sticks	A Ram Sam Sam [Karaoke], Chicken Lips and Lizard Hips
Rule #7: Use What You've Been Given	On Top of Spaghetti, We're Gonna Rock Around the Clock Tonight
Rule #8: Feel Free To Create	D'yer Maker, Coconut
Rule #9: Use More Than Your Mind	A Hundred Bottles of Milk, Runaway
Rule #10: Learning Is Your Friend	A Ram Sam Sam [Karaoke], Tutti Frutti, By the Light of the Silvery Moon
Rule #11: Keep The Learning Pleasant	Who Stole the Cookies?, Boogie Woogie Bugle Boy, Wooly Bully
Rule #12: The Rhythm's In Yourself	Surfin' Bird, Swinging on a Star, You Can't Roller Skate in a Buffalo Herd
Rule #13: Keep The Brain Cells Working	Footloose

REFERENCE PAGES

Plurals

If a noun ends in "-s," "-sh," "-ch," "-x," or "-z," the plural is formed by adding "es." Here are some examples:

moss	--	mosses
wish	--	wishes
dish	--	dishes
watch	--	watches
fox	--	foxes
whiz	--	whizzes

With nouns ending in "y," we usually change the "y" to "i" and add "es." Here are some examples:

city	--	cities
baby	--	babies
country	--	countries

However, if "y" is preceded by a vowel, we add "s" to form the plural. Some examples are:

turkey	--	turkeys
monkey	--	monkeys

Irregular Plural Nouns

If a noun ends in "-f" or "-fe," most of the time we just add "s" to form the plural. For instance:

belief	--	beliefs
chief	--	chiefs

With irregular nouns that end in "-f," we change the "-f" to "ve" and add "es." Here are some examples:

knife	--	knives
half	--	halves
leaf	--	leaves
self	--	selves

To make a plural of nouns ending with "o" preceded by a consonant, we add "es." For example:

hero	--	heroes
potato	--	potatoes

However, if the "o" is preceded by a vowel, we just add "s." For instance:

radio	--	radios
video	--	videos

Finally, with compound words, the plural is formed by making the base noun plural:

brother-in-law	--	brothers-in-law
mother-in-law	--	mothers-in-law

List of Irregular Nouns in the Plural:

basis	—	bases
child	—	children
crisis	—	crises
criterion	—	criteria
deer	—	deer
foot	—	feet
goose	—	geese
index	—	indices
louse	—	lice
man	—	men
medium	—	media
mouse	—	mice
ox	—	oxen
piano	—	pianos
radius	—	radii
salmon	—	salmon
species	—	species
stimulus	—	stimulii
sheep	—	sheep
tooth	—	teeth
trout	—	trout
woman	—	women

Synonyms

The following is a list of common synonyms, words that mean approximately the same thing:

ability	–	talent	invent	–	create
about	–	almost, nearly	job	–	work
accident	–	mishap	large	–	huge
achievement	–	accomplishment	law	–	rule
agree	–	consent	love	–	passion
anger	–	displeasure	near	–	neighboring
answer	–	respond	price	–	cost
ask	–	request	quick	–	swift
bizarre	–	weird	quiet	–	silent
bother	–	irritate	religion	–	faith
brave	–	courageous	report	–	declare
cheap	–	inexpensive	same	–	equivalent
correct	–	true	see	–	perceive
crazy	–	mad	shape	–	design
do	–	perform	show	–	demonstrate
enemy	–	foe	sly	–	sneaky
fair	–	just	spirit	–	energy
fat	–	plump	stay	–	remain
fight	–	quarrel	story	–	narration
fix	–	repair	strange	–	abnormal
friend	–	companion	strict	–	severe
game	–	sport	strong	–	powerful
good	–	honorable	stupid	–	dull
happy	–	cheerful	sure	–	positive
hard	–	difficult	surprise	–	astonishment
hate	–	despise	swift	–	speedy
help	–	assist	take	–	grab
hit	–	beat	teach	–	instruct
holy	–	saintly	travel	–	trip
honest	–	truthful	try	–	attempt
hurt	–	injure	wide	–	spacious
important	–	significant	wise	–	intelligent

Antonyms

The following is a list of common antonyms, words that represent opposites.

add	–	subtract	light	–	dark
all	–	none	long	–	short
always	–	never	lost	–	found
back	–	front	loud	–	soft
before	–	after	love	–	hate
begin	–	end	many	–	few
big	–	little	more	–	less
black	–	white	morning	–	evening
boy	–	girl	most	–	least
come	–	go	near	–	far
day	–	night	new	–	old
dead	–	alive	old	–	new
empty	–	full	on	–	off
fast	–	slow	open	–	close
fat	–	thin	over	–	under
find	–	lose	same	–	different
first	–	last	sharp	–	dull
floor	–	ceiling	small	–	large
friend	–	enemy	something	–	nothing
give	–	get	start	–	stop
go	–	stop	tall	–	short
good	–	bad	then	–	now
happy	–	sad	to	–	from
heaven	–	hell	top	–	bottom
heavy	–	light	up	–	down
high	–	low	wet	–	dry
in	–	out	yes	–	no
left	–	right			

COMMON IRREGULAR VERBS

The following is a list of common irregular verbs.

Infinitive	Simple Past Tense	Past Participle
to be	was/were	been
to beat	beat	beaten
to become	became	become
to begin	began	begun
to bend	bent	bent
to bet	bet	bet
to bite	bit	bitten
to bleed	bled	bled
to blow	blew	blown
to break	broke	broken
to bring	brought	brought
to broadcast	broadcast	broadcast
to build	built	built
to burst	burst	burst
to buy	bought	bought
to catch	caught	caught
to choose	chose	chosen
to come	came	come
to cost	cost	cost
to cut	cut	cut
to dig	dug	dug
to do	did	done
to draw	drew	drawn
to drive	drove	driven
to eat	ate	eaten
to fall	fell	fallen
to feed	fed	fed
to feel	felt	felt
to fight	fought	fought
to find	found	found
to fly	flew	flown
to forecast	forecast	forecast
to forget	forgot	forgotten
to forgive	forgave	forgiven

Infinitive	Simple Past Tense	Past Participle
to freeze	froze	frozen
to get	got	gotten
to give	gave	given
to go	went	gone
to grow	grew	grown
to hang	hung	hung
to have	had	had
to hear	heard	heard
to hide	hid	hidden
to hit	hit	hit
to hold	held	held
to hurt	hurt	hurt
to keep	kept	kept
to know	knew	known
to lay	laid	laid
to lead	led	led
to leave	left	left
to lend	lent	lent
to let	let	let
to lie	lay	lain
to light	lit/lighted	lit/lighted
to lose	lost	lost
to make	made	made
to mean	meant	meant
to meet	met	met
to mistake	mistook	mistaken
to pay	paid	paid
to put	put	put
to quit	quit	quit
to read	read	read
to ride	rode	ridden
to ring	rang	rung
to rise	rose	risen
to run	ran	run
to say	said	said
to see	saw	seen
to seek	sought	sought
to sell	sold	sold
to send	sent	sent

Infinitive	Simple Past Tense	Past Participle
to set	set	set
to shake	shook	shaken
to shine	shine/shined	shone/shined
to shoot	shot	shot
to shrink	shrank	shrunk
to shut	shut	shut
to sing	sang	sung
to sit	sat	sat
to sleep	slept	slept
to slide	slid	slid
to speak	spoke	spoken
to speed	sped	sped
to spend	spent	spent
to spit	spat	spat
to split	split	split
to spread	spread	spread
to spring	sprang	sprung
to stand	stood	stood
to steal	stole	stolen
to stick	stuck	stuck
to sting	stung	stung
to stink	stank	stunk
to strike	struck	struck/stricken
to swear	swore	sworn
to sweep	swept	swept
to swim	swam	swum
to swing	swang	swung
to take	took	taken
to teach	taught	taught
to tear	tore	torn
to tell	told	told
to think	thought	thought
to throw	threw	thrown
to understand	understood	understood
to upset	upset	upset

Infinitive	Simple Past Tense	Past Participle
to wake	woke	woken
to wear	wore	worn
to weave	wove	woven
to weep	wept	wept
to win	won	won
to wind	wound	wound
to write	wrote	written

Modals

The following is a list of commonly used modals:

> can
> could
> had better
> may
> might
> must
> ought to
> shall
> should
> will
> would

Other similar expressions that function as modals are:

> "be" + able to   [like **can**]
> "be" + going to   [like **will**]
> "be" + supposed to
> have to
> have got to
> used to

NOTES:

    1.   No final "-s" is added to modals when the subject is he, she, or it. Example: He **can** do it.

    2.   Modals are followed by the simple form of the verb. The same example illustrates this: He can **do** it.

HOMONYMS

ball	–	bawl	horse	–	hoarse	see	–	sea

ball – bawl horse – hoarse see – sea
beat – beet hour – our seem – seam
blue – blew I – eye sew – sow, so
board – bored knight – night soar – sore
brake – break meat – meet stake – steak
buy – by one – won sun – son
cent – scent pail – pale Sunday – sundae
clothes – close pain – pane tea – tee
cot – caught pear – pair tide – tied
eight – ate plane – plain toe – tow
hair – hare rap – wrap waist – waste
heal – heel rode – road wait – weight
him – hymn sale – sail write – right

PRESENT PERFECT

The present perfect verb tense expresses the idea of something either happening or not happening sometime before now. An example might be:

Where has your mama gone?

Another use for the present perfect is expressing the repetition of some activity before now. For example:

"I have studied English everyday from 9 a.m. until 11 a.m."

Finally, when we use "for" or "since" to describe a situation that began in the past and continues until now, we use the present perfect tense. For example:

I have studied English for five months.